BASIC COMMON CENT$

A beginner's guide toward financial literacy

SPENCER J. SEITZ

Publisher's Information

EBookBakery Books

Author contact: spencer.j.seitz@ampf.com

ISBN 978-1-953080-21-9

Acknowledgments

Thanks to all those people who have helped form and guide my life, perspective, and career. Starting with my grandparents, parents and their friends. Pastors Ensign, Schultz, and Forsberg, over my lifetime. All the people of the Wakefield Rotary Club.

Special thanks to Michael Neri who taught me much more than how to run a business and of course the greatest gift in my life of my lovely bride of 37 years who has not only saved my life but the lives of others.

Dedication

This book is dedicated to those who work to help others.

Contents

Understanding and Building on Your Strengths........................ 1
Acquiring Money and Wealth.. 4
Building a Network.. 9
Determine What is Important to You.................................... 12
Spending Your Money.. 19
Using Debt Properly... 23
Retirement Saving.. 29
The Magic Formula.. 31
Saving and Investing.. 37
Savings Vehicles vs. Investment Vehicles.............................. 41
Taxes.. 46
The Why and When of Insurance.. 48
Buying vs. Leasing a Car.. 52
Buying a Home vs. Renting.. 56
Bringing it All Together.. 57
About the Author... 60

Forward

My father encouraged me to leave everything better than we found it.

Since each day moves me 24 hours closer to my exit from this world, that challenge becomes more time sensitive.

I'm a Financial Advisor and I keep hearing that financial inequality is at the core of what's wrong in our country; that many kids from challenged environments are unable to excel as they don't have the opportunity to become financially literate early in life. This may be true but based on my experience many people don't grasp basic financial concepts until later in life if ever.

Knowledge is Power

The old fable of two friends walking through the woods when they spot a bear applies here. The older friend stops to tie his shoes upon spotting the bear while the other comments "Do you think you can outrun him?". The older friend replies "Nope! I only have to outrun you".

Moral: You will never have complete knowledge of all things financial, but the more you know compared to what others know, the better your chance of success.

This book is derived from my experiences over a lifetime. I have created and run four successful businesses and had three corporate positions. Several of my ventures were successful. One wasn't. There have been times in my life I have been invited to some of the most exclusive venues in America. But there have also been times that I have actively sought "road-kill" for my next meal. I was blessed to grow up in comfortable, safe homes. Yet twice I've had to defend my family by presenting deadly force. So, I've experienced a lot, and it's given me an ability to empathize with people from many walks of life.

I didn't write this book for personal financial benefit. My plan is to direct all profits from sales to The Dawn Foundation. The goal of the Dawn Foundation is to "Support Those Who Help Others". My goal is to create more successful people, who in turn will help others in need. Let's 'pay it forward' and by doing so, we may all participate in leaving this world a better place.

Spencer Seitz, 2021

INTRODUCTION

Both land mines and gold mines lie ahead. Most aren't labeled but you'll know which is which if you pay attention. I'll help you identify and avoid the former and capture all the gold you can.

Avoiding financial landmines is a huge part of success. Financial pitfalls not only drain away your money, but they waste your time, place stress on your emotions, and distract you from profitable opportunities. If you live in the United States, I can assure you there will be opportunities but the number of them that cross your path will not be unlimited. Be alert or someone else will take them.

The impacts of financial landmines aren't limited to a loss of money. They impact the very quality of your life. Financial stresses burden us with anxiety which, like a stone dropped in a pool, ripples and affects everyone around us. Stress impacts your relationships and how you interact with others.

If you are upset or angry the tendency to make illogical or emotional decisions increases. This is a nice way of saying you may not be someone that others wish to be around, and you are more likely to make bad choices.

Avoid life's tempting distractions, the pitfalls everyone faces and plan for tomorrow even though that's not always easy. Remember the Staples Office Supply chain's ad campaign that featured "The Easy Button"? You just push the button and the things you need magically appear. The problem is that there is no "easy button". Success comes from the goals you define followed by hard work and years of working toward those goals. And how we define success isn't the same for everyone.

I had a high school friend whose goal was to work at an auto plant stamping parts. It was a tough, dirty job. 40 years later he is retired, and he is a happy grandpa. He accomplished his dream, has had a great life, raised and supported a family, and is now comfortably retired. Our goals may not be the same, but my friend is a successful man.

Financial Literacy

Financial literacy should help you attain financial security. Financial security will position you to:

1. Leave an abusive spouse
2. Start your own business
3. Better provide for your family
4. Be able to change jobs
5. Be able to move to a new town
6. Help others

1

Understanding & Building on Your Strengths

Life is not fair! Okay, get over it.

Guess what. You're going to face all kinds of challenges. We all do. But before you curl up in the corner with an anxiety attack, consider all the advantages you have. Do that and with a bit of effort you can flip the fact that life isn't fair and make it work to your advantage.

I have friends from church who fled to America years ago to build a better life. They arrived with little yet accomplished so much, and their children are achieving even more. How? They made the effort to achieve. What drove them to succeed? In their case, having fled the hardship and bloodshed of a civil war gave them the perspective that the "challenges" we face in America are not that challenging.

They faced other obstacles too. The wife of one of those friends has dementia. The husband works 50 hours a week, drives 2 hours a day to and from work, and still has time to care for his family. He always has a smile, shows concern for others, and is one of the greatest people I know. His faith supports him, and his positive attitude is something we can all strive for.

Another friend, American born, started work at age 14 to support his parents and a sister. When he went to high school, he carefully planned his absences to work so he could provide for his family and still graduate. When challenged by a guidance counselor advising him, he could only miss 3 more days or he wouldn't graduate my friend responded "I know! I have bills to pay and family to feed. I will be missing 2 of those days." He knew what he had to do, and did what it took to succeed. He had a plan and goals to allocate his time to achieve his goals.

Dr Singh is a retired cardiac surgeon in Rhode Island. He was born in India, worked through Dyslexia and Attention Deficit Disorder, suffered terrible injuries as a child, learned a second language, overcame racism, and became one of the most respected surgeons in the country.

Okay, so most of us don't start life with the massive challenges my friends faced. There will always be someone who had it easier than you, but don't overlook how fortunate you are compared to many others.

First Advantage: I grew up in a family of hard working, successful parents, and grandparents. I came from a relatively modest background, but I had an important advantage - a Grandfather who showed me the value of work. What he taught me wasn't rocket science. He showed me how to push a broom, wield a paintbrush, and how to shovel. My father introduced me to the lawn mower, a wheelbarrow, and an ax. These skills were basic, but they were important. They gave me tools that helped me begin working towards my financial security. Even more important, they taught me the importance of a good work ethic.

The Generational Advantage

Having parents and grandparents that can teach you how to work, and be an example on other life issues, is beneficial. But if you don't have this benefit, consider it your responsibility to create that advantage for your future family.

"Grandparents are easy to shop for, whatever you get them, it's exactly what they wanted."

Second advantage: Not all Americans have access to tools and to folks who can teach how to use them. But most young people have internet access, and there you can find training for hundreds of skills. Don't pass up any opportunity if someone offers to teach the tricks of skilled or unskilled labor. But lacking that, remember Google, YouTube and the hundreds of other online resources. They are your second advantage.

Third advantage: There is a third advantage, and it's a way of thinking that really helps. I call it, "avoiding stupid". It can be the greatest advantage of them all. This advantage is incredibly obvious, will save you time, money, and stress, and none of us use it as well as we should. Hopefully you can learn from my mistakes.

2

Acquiring Money and Wealth

Before we look at how to manage money, you have to accumulate some. You'll need a job. And to be employed, you need to offer value to an employer. The more value you offer, the more you'll get paid. So, let's focus on how to be more valuable.

You need a job, of course, so ask yourself, "What is my potential boss looking for? Empathize with him or her. Empathy is normally a term used to understand a hardship someone else is experiencing. But apply it to the person who might hire you.

Hiring good people is hard and takes special talents. The person doing the hiring often has other responsibilities while he or she is searching for someone with the required skills. They are looking for a good fit between the job and the person they interview. Finding the best person is important to them. They have skin in the game because if they choose the wrong person, they can be harmed financially or by reputation.

Your task during the job interview is to think how your skills can fit the job he or she needs to fill. Learn what is important to the company and how you can serve them well. Let them know you will become good at the job and work hard to be productive. Once you have the job you want, start making yourself valuable. Offer to take on other challenges or learn new skills so others will need you no matter where you work. Start thinking about your future at your present place of employment. Assuming you are great in the job, what is the next step up the ladder?

Your first job is unlikely to be your last. Use it and every job thereafter to learn how to be more valuable. You may discover that your interests are in some other kind of work. That's good to know. If you decide there's limited opportunity with the current position, consider a change of employers.

How much are you worth? There is currently a discussion that the minimum wage is a living wage. Don't accept that. You want more. Make yourself more valuable and you'll acquire better work with better pay and a better life. Think of the minimum wage as nothing more than where you start, not where you want to stay.

I worked with a friend who regularly volunteered to take on projects that needed to get done, even when no one was assigned to do them. The boss could always count on him and knew he was thorough and that the work would be done well and on time. Guess who constantly got promotions. He rose up the ladder and made more and more money. But he earned every position he won by being available, reliable and a worker with a great, positive attitude.

As the economy worsened and layoffs occurred, my friend was the last to lose his job and the first to be rehired. Not only was he the first to be rehired but other businesses approached him as well because of his work reputation.

What Is Your Value?

I was once told you are worth what it costs to replace you. Let's visit both sides of that comment. From an employer's perspective, if they can hire a skilled person at $18/hour why would they pay more? From an employee's perspective, if you are getting paid $13/hour and people are hiring at $18/hour, you need to act. Have a conversation with your current employer and ask them to increase your wage. You may need to change employers to get paid what you are worth.

My first job was burying dead fish in my grandfather's garden. It paid 25 cents an hour when I was nine years old. I quickly learned:

1. the importance of wearing shoes when I shovel
2. I had to take smaller bites of dirt and move faster to keep my job.
3. this was not the career I wanted for life

Treat every job as a challenge to conquer and show your employer how well you can do what they need done. Learn what is important to the company and excel at it. If you make yourself valuable like my friend, your employer or another company will want you too.

Learn what to do and what not to do. Observe how others handle different situations. This kind of learning is available to you every day if you pay attention. And hey, it's free.

In my first job after General Motors, I was ill-prepared to meet the different challenges I faced, and I wasn't productive for the employees who depended on me. Good management could have helped me be better at my job, but in this case poor management and an inefficient work environment led to the failure of the company. I remembered the bad management practices I'd observed when I took my next job, and pledged to God never to use them. The new company was much better managed. We went from failure to success in six months, the people who worked with me shared in that success, and all I had to do was avoid the previous employers' bad practices. Seeing bad examples can be invaluable if you keep a sharp eye out for ways to do better.

Don't forget the basics. Be dependable. Be on time and ready for work every day. Keep a good attitude. When it is time to select someone for a promotion, the person who remembers these basics has a better chance of improving their position.

When it's time to move on from your current job, be smart. Always be looking for your next chance for advancement. Don't announce that you're looking, just keep your eyes and ears open for opportunities. Think about the pluses and minuses of your current position so that when it's time to make a change, you'll have a head start. Keep on good terms and leave in a friendly fashion when it's time to move on. Don't burn bridges. Many industries are small worlds and you're likely to run into old colleges as you move up the ladder. It never hurts if most of them think well of you. Remember the old saying, "The people you meet on the way up the ladder may be the ones to catch you on the way down." Treat everyone with the respect a fellow worker deserves.

You are perceived as more valuable if you are currently working when you interview for a new job. I can't overstate how much of an advantage having a job is when you interview. Protect the job you have until you have secured one you prefer. Don't speak poorly of your current employer to a prospective new employer. Bad mouthing an old boss never makes you look good. If offered a job, discuss the need to give your old employer adequate notice that you will be leaving. Depending on the position you have, two weeks notice is average. These are all considerations that make you more valuable, cost nothing, and only require minimal effort.

Don't be a MEMAW. A MEMAW is a person who exerts Minimum Effort for Maximum Wage. These people are easily spotted and disliked by everyone they work with. They rarely get promoted. Keep your distance from them. They will teach you bad habits, slow you down, and even worse you may be considered a MEMAW by association.

"When I said, 'I want you to sleep on it'. I meant when you go home tonight."

Once you identify a career that you would like, pursue it. This could require changing employers and most careers will have extra training or certifications. Go get them. Yes, it requires effort and sacrifice but think of yourself as a business you are building, and invest in yourself.

Work is a Competitive Environment.

As a graduating senior I remember sleeping outside in a line overnight to sign up for a job interview. February in Northern Michigan is a bit cool but these were desperate times. As one of the successful candidates for an interview, I was given a description of the job. Being good at math I quickly calculated that the cost of business clothing and a car required for the job was greater than the annual compensation. I passed my interview spot to the next person.

A friend of my father's got me an interview at General Motors. He coached me as I hope I am coaching you on how to handle myself. It didn't happen overnight but six months and four interviews later I was offered a job. With a bachelor's degree in marketing and a minor in accounting and management, I was overqualified for the only job available – to file letters in alphabetical order. With the local unemployment rate at nearly 30%, I was happy to have the work and get a foot in the door. But three years and four promotions later, I had learned the large corporate world was not for me, better opportunities existed, and it was time to move on.

Just recently a friend's child graduated from one of the most prestigious schools in the country, yet couldn't find a job. His sister had a friend in the field he wanted to enter. He welcomed the help, got hired and is now very successful. Look for help along the way as you explore job opportunities. And, when you are successful yourself, be there to help others seeking a better position. In other words, 'pay it forward'.

Even with all the job postings on the internet today, it's invaluable to have a friend inside a company who will give you a recommendation.

3

Building a Network

If you want friends, be a friend. The next ten people you're nice to may not become friends. You will help others and some will never reciprocate. But there is a world of great people out there. Make the effort to find them. When things are tough, you'll be happy to discover that your real friends are there for you.

Friends come from everywhere. You'll make them from school buddies, previous and current coworkers, at social activities, church, community service clubs and projects you volunteer for. You'll meet some at shared activities like golf or shooting. Friends lead you to more friends if you share yourself with others. And once you have kids, many of your friends will be the parents of your children's friends.

Social media allows you to keep in touch with friends and coworkers without geographic restraints. Don't be afraid to reach out to someone you worked with years ago to ask for guidance on applying for a job at their company. This is business, and it's perfectly acceptable to ask for an introduction or a recommendation—with one caveat. Be prepared to be just as helpful to others.

Put yourself out there. You won't make quality friends hiding in your mother's basement playing video games and getting stoned. A friend's son recently received a fantastic summer internship. Over 10,000 people applied and while highly qualified, the odds weren't in his favor. But it turned out the president of the company had a son who played soccer with my friends' son. That contact helped him get the job. In the real world, as competitive as it is today, it takes more than just being qualified to win a fantastic job. Get out in the world and get involved. It's not hard, and it's fun. You'll meet some great people because surprisingly, a lot of the people are also looking for friends.

When you get the chance to help a friend, be a superstar. Go all out. I lost my job in the 80's when the company I worked for closed because of poor management. Times were bad, but tough times help you discover who your real friends are. I also made sure I helped those who helped me so they were glad they had when they needed a friend.

When I made my last career change, I reached out to 104 friends and associates whom I had helped over the years. The purpose of my call was to tell them about my new career in hopes they might know someone who could use my services. One hundred of the people I called scheduled meetings with me immediately. Two scheduled time in the next couple weeks and two would not return my call. After I became successful in my new career, both of the two that wouldn't return my call reached out to me asking for business. Needless to say, I choose to devote my attention to those who were there to help me.

Building networks of friends and associates takes time and effort. If you can have fun and support your community doing it, so much the better.

The Rule of 52

I am uncertain if this is a real rule or a trick adults used to get me to work longer. In any case, growing up I was told the standard was that you needed to be productive 52 hours a week to be successful. Working, learning, or helping others all counted as productive time.

Some people learn from books, some learn they did something wrong by watching others. Still others learn by getting involved and helping. What's important is keeping pressure on yourself to learn something new every day.

One of the best learning opportunities comes from serving your community. The Community Service people you volunteer with can be great sources of knowledge. They provide on-the-job training and expose you to different skills. At the same time, they offer different perspectives on the issues you deal with. What's more, the people you support make it easier to see how lucky you've been. Helping them assures that you won't take for granted the opportunities you've been given.

There is no shortage of problems in the world and helping solve them creates huge community service opportunities. Devote time to issues you care about. You'll stay involved and find the work emotionally rewarding. Service groups like the Rotary and Lions Clubs provide help for a lot of worthy organziations. Churches offer specific help for people you know in your community. Working to reduce hunger, domestic violence, homelessness, or child abuse are all good causes with an unending need for help. Conservation efforts are another area that can always use your help.

The causes you get involved in are important, but the fact that you get involved is more important. It is easy to spout off about all the things wrong in the world. But problems only get solved by people who roll up their sleeves and go to work.

Use your skills. If you are a teacher, tutor kids that need help. There is a huge demand for mental health care if you have the skills to volunteer. If you have skills in that area, volunteering a few hours a week could save lives. We take clean water for granted, but keeping our water safe is a critical issue. Working the phones at a helpline or picking up trash at the beach all make a difference.There's plenty of important ways to contribute.

4

Determine What is Important to You

An early step in building your personal version of a great life is to determine what's important to you. Your goals will change over time, but spend some time now thinking about your priorities. Set goals around them. I made the mistake of not setting goals for myself. I was afraid that if I didn't reach my goal, I'd think of myself as a failure. With no goal, I figured I couldn't fail.

I came to realize that with no goal you have no direction. Think of a boat with no rudder that wanders but never makes port. Without a destination you can easily get off course. You'll do nonproductive things. Decide what's important to you and making decisions gets much easier.

Having clear goals will help you focus your energy on reaching them. It's competitive out there. We all fight for a share of limited dollars, the resource you need to accomplish many of your goals. Maybe you want a car, have an urge to vacation or a need to pay medical bills. Maybe you'd like to host a party this weekend or help a friend in desperate need. As certain as the sun will rise, you're going to face constant demands on your finances. Even if you're as successful as a Gates, Bezos, or Buffet, demands on your savings will never top. But think how much easier it will be if you have a plan on where and how to spend your money and you know what you're saving for.

With goals determined, you now have direction and with direction, decision making becomes easier. Is it more important to pay my health insurance or get a new tattoo?

It is your life so these are your decisions. There are some glaringly obvious mistakes you can avoid, and I would like to highlight those through the "D's of Stupid."

The D's of Stupidity

"Implementing these changes won't be easy. We're pretty set in doing things the wrong way."

We all do stupid things. Some of us do them repeatedly. It's where the term "you can't fix stupid" comes from. The best we can do is to avoid doing stupid things while keeping our distance from folks who do 'stupid' with great regularity.

Stupid is simple to identify. You've seen the guy screaming at his son's little league coach; the person who hits their spouse; the ones who speak poorly of others because of race, sex, gender preference, or religion. You know the neighbor who lets their dog bark twelve hours a day while his neighbor's wife is recovering from radiation treatments. The world has an endless supply of stupid. When you encounter someone who fits the description, learn from them and avoid making the same mistakes.

There is no vaccine to defend against stupidity, and natural selection has yet to eliminate it. Why we encounter so much of it is beyond my pay grade, but I am confident you'll have to deal with stupid in your lifetime.

D<u>**D**</u>**rugs** is the first of them and the most harmful. There are great jobs just waiting for workers today, but many can't be filled because the qualified employees can't pass the drug test. Really! People applying for these jobs know they'll be tested, yet they can't stop their hunger for a high long enough to get hired for a dream job that could propel them and their families to financial security.

Drugs are often illegal, and it sure doesn't look good at the job interview when you explain that the employment gap on your resume relates to jail time you did. It'll haunt you for a long, long time, and with social media you can bet a potential employer will find out if you have a history of using. Despite temptations to take them, stay away.

As a quick aside, many people suffer from social anxiety or feel overwhelmed by challenges they face. The community service work I do has shown me that my own problems are pretty small when I set them in perspective against a world of suffering that exists. Next time you feel things are tough, take a few minutes and go to www.waterforcambodia.org. It will help set your personal challenges in a global context, and you'll feel better equipped to handle them.

Drinking. Drinking is part of our social fabric if you don't overdo it. People become more vocal when they drink which creates a great listening opportunity if you stay sober. You can get to know others in moments when they are less socially masked. Observing how they act also shows you how to behave, and how not to behave at important social or business functions. I rarely drink at business functions (club soda with a lime usually stops people from asking why I am not drinking), and I'm often the designated driver.

Most of us will have a drink, and how much we drink is a personal matter… to a degree. Obviously, you've gone too far if you get slapped with a DUI. Consider the time and cost of that kind of stupid. Legal fees can set you back $10,000. Then figure the time you'll spend in court, and your lost wages. Your insurance cost will skyrocket, and if you have a job that requires a driver's license, you could lose your job.

Next, look at the hidden costs of a DUI. Future employers may see it as a red flag; that you've identified yourself as stupid. If two candidates with similar qualifications apply for the same job, and one doesn't have a criminal record, who do you think gets hired?

I haven't mentioned the harm you could cause to yourself or others. Maybe insurance covers the physical damage, but what if you, a passenger, or a person you hit suffers lifetime damage. That is a burden that is yours forever.

When I worked for General Motors, I was one of three junior mangers who attended an executive level event, and we had too much to drink. We decided we'd educate the top executive of our division on how things should be done. Fortunately, a mid-level manager named Larry put his hand on my shoulder and advised me to "stay". My career flourished from that point. The two other junior managers who did 'educate' the top brass got assigned to "Siberia". *Thank you, Larry.*

Divorce. The most important decision you will make in your life is who you marry, live with, or take as a life partner. The benefit of having a trusted loving partner to create a better life with is immeasurable. Sorry, but I have already claimed the greatest woman in the world for myself, but there are still awesome people out there. By the grace of god, I have been very successful in making that most important decision of my life. While I'm not qualified to offer in-depth advice on who you select, I urge you to be careful about your choice.

Divorce has a devastating effect on everybody involved. The emotional cost is usually great, and the financial cost will be significant. I can offer a bit of advice about staying married. Many years ago, the pastor at church gave a sermon on the most successful marriages. He told us about a recurring theme he'd discovered when speaking with long-married couples. It's as simple as it is profound. "Do something nice for your spouse every day".

It works and here's my theory of why. First, if you are doing something nice for someone everyday it is easier for them to forgive you when you do something stupid … and you will. We all do. Second, if your focus is on doing something nice, you'll spend less time annoying your partner by doing something stupid.

Drama may be a surprising topic for behavior that can damage your finances, but it can.

A recent Harvard graduate posted a video on social media suggesting she was going to stab the next person who disagreed with her on a certain subject. She threatened to stand over them while they bled out. While I am confident this was just theatre, the internationally respected company she had an internship with couldn't take the risk and immediately terminated her internship.

I mentioned how helpful it is to imagine yourself in the position of the hiring manger. Would you want to be the person responsible for having hired someone who publicly threatened violence? How well would someone who did that reflect on the company? Would you want them working next to you? Heaven forbid if the person hurt a coworker or a client and you were responsible for hiring them. It's a burden the manager could bear for life.

Adding fuel to the fire, after the Harvard graduate lost her internship, she went back online and stated how mean the employer was for terminating her. She blamed them. Really? Wasn't she the one threatening to stab people? It is hard for me to think her actions would make her attractive to any elite business.

Knuckleheads. Don't be one. Yes, I know the word Knucklehead does not start with a **D** but the word I would like to use is not acceptable to my editor. The world is smaller now that everyone has a camera on their phone. An unnecessary burst of anger or arrogance can now be preserved forever. It could define you in ways that aren't complimentary, and the image can hang on for years. Though knucklehead behavior isn't productive, you see happening daily.

Recently a local ice cream store had to close a location because the "adult" clients constantly threatened the kids scooping ice cream behind the counter. The kids were told to refuse service to anyone who wouldn't wear a mask in a time of pandemic. By bullying young kids, the customers put their own immaturity on display. They also shut down the ice cream store for all who came to enjoy it.

Decisions. We make decisions every day. Rest assured, none of us make all the correct decisions.

The best you can do is to gather the information you have at the time and make your best choice. The danger in decision making is that we are emotional creatures, and many times our feelings creep into our decisions. In addition to being emotional about our choice, the ability to gather good data can be challenging.

In your work environment, hopefully you have data you can trust. In a society where news has become entertainment, getting solid data is getting harder. Sometimes news contains 'facts' presented in a way to be attractive to the audience it targets. The internet contains reams of information. Some of it is real and some of it is 'fake news' creatively invented. Bad data almost always generates bad decisions. Develop trusted and credible sources and continue to monitor them for bias. Good luck!

When emotion gets involved in decision making, it can cloud clear thinking. A friend of mine and I once considered buying a very cool local sporting goods store offering kayaks, archery equipment, and fishing gear. Look at the benefits. We'd have access to all the cool stuff we could ever want; we'd associate with great people and work in a fun environment. Both of us have strong yet different financial backgrounds that gave credibility to our decision. Forging ahead seemed like a no brainer. What could go wrong? We were so excited about the business that we looked right past the fact that it couldn't be profitable. The local market was already saturated with too much competition. Fortunately, my friend's wife firmly brought that reality to our attention.

Finally, when it comes to making the right choice, often the answer isn't clear. So, uncertain, you put making the decision on hold. Don't. Not deciding is the same as deciding no. It is okay to decide not to take action or make a change, but do it in a conscious manner and move on with life. When it's time to choose, assemble the facts and make the best decision you can based on the information you have.

Remember also that not every decision has to be set in stone. Monitor how your choice is going and if it looks like you made the wrong choice, see if you can do an about face. There's nothing wrong with making the wrong choice if you follow it with corrective action.

5

Spending Your Money

Okay! So now that we've focused on building character and an attitude for success, let's put theory behind us and get to the nuts and bolts of building your personal assets.

Terms like Investment Selection, Rates of Return, and Asset Allocation are all important. But they mean nothing if your account balance is zero. We have to start making money and building assets. And the first rule to build wealth is make and save money. It's the simplest and most violated concept in personal finance; the need to spend less than you make. We all know that, but did you know that the average American only has life savings adequate to cover a $2,000 expense? A single financial emergency can blow that away.

Sure, that new face piercing is important and that your i-Phone is a generation behind the newest model is a complete embarrassment, but wouldn't it be nice to have cash available to get medicine for your sick child? There will always be temptations pulling at your money. Be mature enough to identify what's important to you and spend or save accordingly.

Buying rounds at the bar to be a big shot in front of your friends may look good in the movies and may make you feel important. But when you can't pay off your credit card, and start paying 2% a month interest, nobody from the bar will be calling to help pay off your bill.

As sure as you breathe, you'll be spending every day. The trick to meeting the savings goals we will discuss is to learn the keys to spending smart. If you pay attention to how you buy, you also increase your ability to save.

Every day you hear of a great deal on something that you might need. Ask, is it really a deal or is everybody without a coupon overpaying? Use coupons. RETAIL ME NOT is a helpful app. There are others.

Take the emotion out of the buying decision. Ask - *Is this something I want or something I need?* If it is something you want, it will take money away from your savings goals. Ask - *Is it important enough to take money from my savings?* If "yes" then make the purchase.

Amazon is a great place to find everything. Keep in mind that they are providing few local jobs and even less in local taxes. If you don't support local community stores to some degree, you won't have local jobs.

Without getting political, buying American-Made products may cost a little more, but we're discovering more about the unseen costs of depending on other countries for manufacturing. Purchasing goods manufactured outside the U.S. means fewer jobs for your family, neighbors, friends and maybe yourself. I am not proposing we stop buying all foreign products, but when possible, buying American might be in your long-term best interest.

If you have a credit card that offers you rewards like points or discounts, use it as much as possible. Credit cards carry a cost to the retailer of around 2%. That is figured into the price of pretty much everything for sale. If you don't use a credit card for retail purchases, then you are paying the 2% and receiving no benefit. At the same time, pay your card balance off in full every month so you don't get hit with excessive interest charges.

> You may find credit cards are not excepted on large purchases like cars or if used will carry a surcharge for things like college tuition. I had friends who earned large amounts of frequent flier miles by using credit cards to make college tuition payments. The colleges figured this out and now have a 2-3% surcharge if tuition is paid by credit card. If you have to pay a surcharge to use a card, it usually is no longer attractive to use a credit card.

Don't use a credit card if you can't afford to buy the item. Credit cards are a means of payment and not a means of financing except in a real emergency.

Create a budget

So, you need to plan how to spend by having a budget. It's a topic that requires thought and one many others have addressed. But here's what I think are the important points. Don't spend more than you make. Save a portion of every check for your emergency fund and your retirement fund. If you hope to make a big purchase like buying a car or a home, start saving for it now. If you're young, it's hard to think way down the road to the money you'll need for retirement or an emergency. But you will need the money, and there's no time like now to start to plan.

Recently the percentage of income that the average American saves has skyrocketed. It seems counterintuitive when so many have hit the wall of hard times. The reason for the increase in savings is that the virus has increased our awareness that we can't always predict the unexpected. Bad times can surprise us. So many have responded by saving more. Saving is also easier with less opportunity to spend on things like travel and entertainment.

It is okay to enjoy the luxuries of life. Just make sure the most important priority is you. By starting early and saving responsibly for retirement, you will be able to wake up one day and say, "I am going to work because I want to." This is a luxury not everyone will have, so take control of your life and start planning your finances now.

An Emergency Fund

There are few guarantees in life, but one I am certain of is that you will experience an emergency or several. As you build assets, an emergency fund is important for two reasons. First, you're eventually going to need it. Second, if you don't have one, you'll have to get the money from somewhere. That can mean having to siphon from your retirement savings which will cost you in penalties and taxes when you can least afford them. Or it means getting a costly loan or adding credit card debt. In any case, not being prepared for an emergency can become a slippery financial slope.

I have friends in New York who are successful entertainers. They recognized the importance of an emergency fund because as entertainers their incomes fluctuate so often. With the Covid crash this year, their ability to perform and earn a living has been all but eliminated. Their expenses keep coming. To add to their burden, they have twins going into college next fall. But because of their years of planning and saving for college costs, it won't be an insurmountable problem.

Often the emergencies you will face won't be so big. An unexpected car repair, helping get a friend out of jail, or replacing a water heater are more typical. Even though these emergencies are small, they are critical. You'll face much less stress if you have 'rainy day' cash saved up to deal with them.

"I just learned that my golden parachute was not properly packed."

Keep emergency funds set aside in your checking or savings account for just such times. As important as it is to save money and even grow it with interest, more important is the fact you can access emergency funds immediately.

6

Using Debt Properly

Credit is a loan you pay back over time plus an interest charge for the loan. The interest rate or the cost of the loan is based on your credit score and your ability to shop for the best loan rate. A poor credit score can cost you hundreds a month in higher interest expense. Think about that. You could waste an entire month's pay over the period of a year if you have lousy credit. Wouldn't you rather spend the money on your family or yourself? So how can you avoid wasting all that money?

Determining someone's credit score can get complicated, but let's keep it simple. Pay all your debts on time. Paying phone bills, student loans, electric bills, car loans, mortgages or rent all reflect on your willingness to pay. Establish a record of consistently paying on time, and you'll earn a higher credit score. Someone who is consistently late earns a lower or poorer score.

"I take it your credit score has gone up?"

At one point in my life I found it more time efficient to pay bills every sixty days. That may have been time efficient, but it cost me all kinds of late fees and damaged my credit score.

Using the calculators at calculator.net, let's do a quick exercise to show the damage a little poor credit can cause. Assume you want to finance $300,000 on a new home for 30 years and your credit is less than great causing you to qualify for a mortgage at 4% vs. the going rate of 3% for those with good credit. The difference in monthly payment is about $168 which is not horrible but will cost you about $60,000 more over the term of the mortgage. Extending this calculation, if you can pay the higher mortgage payment in this example but qualify for the lower payment, you could save the $168 per month in an investment account. Assume that account earned 6% annually over the 30-year term, the account would be worth close to $163,000 dollars. This example shows how discipline in spending and keeping a good credit score can have a long term impact on your lifetime finances.

While your credit score affects the interest rate you receive when borrowing, it can affect other things as well. For example, companies have discovered a strong correlation between credit scores and insurance claims. So, a good credit score could lower what you pay for insurance. The money you save creates savings you can use for other goals. Some employers find a correlation between better employees and better credit scores. If you're competing for a job, this can make a difference.

Landlords always check credit scores. A good score can mean you get a lower rent and a better apartment or pay a lower security deposit.

The expense of credit card debt can be a huge threat to your financial future. Rates vary, but 24% annual rates are more common than you think. Low rates currently are around 6-8% while a savings account at the bank is paying .2%. Falling into credit card debt is a terrible trap that's expensive to escape. Going into credit card debt for an emergency is sometimes necessary. If you've been smart and built an emergency fund, this may not be an issue. Medical problems, the loss of a job, damage to your car are real emergencies. The desire for a new outfit, to go out to dinner, or to buy playoff tickets can surely be tempting, but they are not emergencies, and they aren't worth the harm going into credit card debt does.

"It's cash. It's kind of like a debit card."

Many years ago, I had a friend who told me he'd maxed out his credit cards. I hadn't seen him for a while when he called to suggest we meet for lunch. After lunch, he was quick to grab the tab and paid with his credit card. I asked how he was doing on paying down his debt. He told me he had gotten a loan from Larry the Loan Shark and had paid off his credit cards. It turns out the interest expense going through Larry was lower than the card rate. I am not recommending my friend's strategy, or suggesting you use a loan shark, but it shows you how expensive credit card interest rates can be.

Why is college under the topic of credit? The answer is that college will be one of the largest expenses you make and few of us get through without loans. It can be an incredibly valuable investment of your time and money, or it can be an unnecessary financial burden to carry for the rest of your life.

In my experience, what I learned outside the classroom was as important as what I learned in the classroom. Managing my time, developing my personal skills, being efficient, and creating priorities were all things I learned just by being there. These were lessons I couldn't capture from books.

Very little of what I learned in class applied to my professional life, but in fairness I had no idea where my professional life was going. When I graduated, employers wouldn't consider you for most jobs unless you'd earned a degree. When General Motors hired me, I was promoted over others who were way more qualified, but they did not have a degree. That may not be the way it should be, but it's how things happen in the real world.

The danger of college is that not everyone needs a college degree to pursue their career. Some get a very expensive degree that isn't cost effective. For example, apprenticeships, the trades, and truck drivers are in demand. But many of these jobs can be done well without the time and cost of going to college.

The military is a great option as a starting point in life whether you get a college degree or not. The service teaches discipline, develops skills, offers time to mature and you may get some college funding. The military can be a source of education or provide an awesome first job and a career start.

A friend's son graduated with a great degree in Turf Management and Agriculture. $100,000 in debt, he leaped into his dream job directly from college. What was that job? He wanted to be a fireman. Fireman are needed, and an important profession, but his degree had no impact on his employment.

All college grad's struggle with the expense of becoming independent. Paying rent or mortgages, car payments, insurance, and food can quickly consume a paycheck. Add the burden of an unnecessary $100,000 college loan and the work needed to be financially successful just got much greater.

That $100,000 loan paid back over 20 years at 6% takes $716 a month from his after-tax income. He'll pay $79,084 in interest over the life of the loan. It's money well spent if it advances a career. But it's like swimming tied to an anchor if your degree isn't relevant.

It's crazy to acquire a degree that's not cost effective. Think of yourself as a business. Will the degree you go for be a good investment in the business you're planning?

When you invest in yourself as with any other investment, you need to do it wisely. If you were buying a business that would provide a 20% return on your investment (after paying the interest) and pay you a good wage, then the investment in a degree might be worth considering. That said, you wouldn't make that investment if the rate of return was a negative 5% a year for the next 20 years. Think about a college degree as money well spent…or not.

During the presidential primaries a big topic of discussion was student loans – to forgive them or not. While we are not here to discuss if doing so is a good or bad idea, the topic did bring the plight of a California doctor to my attention via an interview on CNBC.

I did some research and the physician being interviewed was a legitimate physician. She did graduate from a real med school with a specialty in Holistic medicine. She already had a masters in Acupuncture before attending medical school, and her total college debt was about $450,000. This translates to 20 years of loan payments amounting to $3,222 a month.

The doctor's concern in the interview was that she could not pay both her student loan and living expenses. A little more research suggested the average earnings for a person with her specialty was $7,250 a month. After loan payments, if you deduct taxes, car payments, rent, food, clothing and insurance, there is little doubt she couldn't cover her expenses.

I can't criticize the doctor for her choice of specialties, for example her masters in acupuncture. But her example illustrates how spending too much for an education could prove a bad investment. You must weigh the costs against the possible payout.

In certain cases, such as a physician who works for a nonprofit, it may be possible to reduce the loan payment amount, for example by making income-based loan payments, or even to have much of the loan forgiven. This sounds great until you look deeper.

In the case of a loan like our example, the dollar amount forgiven becomes taxable in that year. So, our doctor would have a one-time taxable event in excess of $450,000. The IRS expects payment in full for this amount, or in this case they'll be looking for a payment of about $144,000. The state may have it's hand out as well. The IRS is going to collect that money one way or another and they don't have a tax forgiveness program. What's more, they charge noncompetitive (abusive) interest rates. So be careful!

Loan forgiveness programs have proven difficult for most people to manage. I am no expert on navigating the process, but I encourage you to get professional tax advice before you consider such an option if it's offered.

College is famous for parties and good times and it surely offers both. But if that's your goal, do yourself a favor. You can achieve it for a lot less expense. Get a job, rent an apartment, find some roommates, and have some fun. It'll be much cheaper and easier on your finances in the long run. You will avoid the burden of paying back a college loan that did not make you more valuable.

7

Retirement Savings

It may seem hard to talk about retirement with a person in their twenties, but it is more important than ever to plan for that now. That said a consistent savings plan combined with the advantages of compound interest and tax-free growth when added to a long investment timeframe are very powerful.

In very simple terms, compound interest/growth lets the growth of your investments accumulate and grow themselves. Adding the fact that no taxes are taken to reduce the amount growing adds further benefit to this process.

Go to a site like www.calculator.net/investment and play around with a few different saving scenarios. Time and discipline are powerful allies for you in your financial life, but you need to elect to use them.

More time to accumulate and grow retirement savings is to your advantage, especially when you start at a young age. The day will arrive when you don't want to go to work or perhaps you are physically or mentally unable to work. As a young person you feel indestructible, and retirement isn't on your radar. But trust me, it will be someday.

Retirement funds come from different sources. You can inherit them, marry them, win them, or save them. The first three options have a low probability of occurring and may be out of your control. So, let's focus on the importance of saving.

Traditionally you will use Social Security funds during retirement, or maybe use pension funds. The money you've set aside is what funds the gap between your living expenses and Social Security/Pension. Social Security is having its challenges now, and it's likely to be even more challenged in thirty to forty years. Let's hope it is there for you, but have a contingency plan.

Many complain that our government is spending too much money and the deficit creates a burden for future generations. I agree. But the question is, what are you going to do about it? You can vote for more responsible government or go buy lottery tickets. Both have an equally poor chance of success.

Step one is to train ourselves to be more financially responsible. The second step is to teach our children the same thing. And third step is to try to save money to help our kids and grandkids. Be assured, they will have to face the burden put on them by our excess government spending, and Social Security may not be the answer for young adults in the future.

Pensions are awesome but rarely exist and are becoming even more rare. In most cases the only jobs with pensions are state and federal. Many state pensions are currently underfunded, and that's not likely to improve. It is a real possibility you can work in a job for forty years and when ready to retire, your pension is reduced or it's just not there. This is a terrible thing and should never happen. But it is already happening.

The money you save for retirement is under your control. The pension and Social Security may not be there, but it's more likely that your retirement investment funds will be if you save and manage them properly.

8

The Magic Formula

Golf is a game well-loved by many. But not me. I know the importance of a proper swing, for example. Yet, after 15 years of trying, I can still throw my clubs further than I can hit the ball. I'm simply not good at executing golf basics. Similarly, some folks may know the importance of financial basics, but that doesn't mean they've been able to execute and be disciplined when it comes to creating financial success.

There's a formula for savings that's been promoted by many experts. I think it's a good place to start.

So here we go:

1. Salve 10% of your gross income to your retirement account.
2. Save 10% of your gross income to your emergency fund.
3. Save 10% of your gross income toward that large purchase that is important to you. House, wedding, college, car, etc.

These savings goals seem excessive and will be challenging, but once you have reached the dollar amount for your emergency fund you can stop contributing to it. Same goes for the large purchase goal.

Focus on a long investment horizon and tax-free growth to put money into your retirement account. Once you start to build your retirement fund, leave it there. Equally important, the sooner you start, the greater your benefits.

The two main types of retirement plans are those provided by your employer and by an IRA account. There are options also for the self-employed, but let's start with the assumption that you'll begin as an employee.

If you work for a nonprofit, they will offer a 403b plan. A larger business will have 401k plans. Both plans are similar and usually have an employer match of some kind. As you get started with your early financial plan, these are great. For example, if you work for ABC Company and their 401k has a 3% match, that's as good as getting a 3% tax free raise.

Here is how it works. Let's assume your annual salary is $50,000. If you save $1,500 in your retirement plan, the company will match that contribution by 100%. You will still be short of the formula goal of saving 10%, but you won't be leaving an easy $1,500 dollars on the table.

A common mistake is that people think they've "maxed out" their annual retirement plan contribution once they contribute the same amount as their employer matches. In 2020 the annual maximum contribution for a young person to a 401k is $19,500. That means you could still add $12,000 as a tax sheltered amount in your retirement fund.

In the example above, I show that the government limits how much you can contribute to your tax-free retirement fund in any one year. It's important to take advantage of every tax-free dollar you can "invest" in your retirement. You may not always be able to fund to the government limit, but your goal should be to fully fund your 401k as quickly as you can. Raises and bonuses will help reach your funding goal.

Some choose to cash out their 401k when they leave a job. That's a bad decision and one that causes them to suffer a 10% penalty for early withdrawal. Don't do it.

When you change jobs, you can often leave the 401k with the current provider. Or, you may be able to move your 401k to your next job and do so without penalty. If those options don't work, you can transfer it to an IRA tax/penalty free. Temping as it may be at the time, don't cash out your 401k or 403b unless you are in critical financial distress.

THE TRADITIONAL IRA AND ROTH IRA

It's important to understanding how much you can save taking advantage of good retirement contributions. Contributions to Traditional 401k, 403b, and IRA accounts reduce your taxable income. They increase what you keep and decrease what you hand over to Uncle Sam. They become even more attractive the longer you work because as your income grows, your marginal tax rate increases (the percentage of your income you pay in taxes). How to keep more and pay less in taxes is why it's a great idea to meet with a tax pro to determine your best tax-shelter plans.

A ROTH IRA becomes more attractive if you are taxed at a lower rate. A ROTH IRA doesn't give you a tax deduction for your retirement contribution, but it has a different benefit. It grows tax free, and when you retire, you get to take out your savings - tax free. Over the course of your employment, tax rates will probably go up. Many years from now you could have a bucket of money that you've saved, and it can be withdrawn tax free.

Ask your tax specialist about 401ks, SEPs, Simples, 457s, 403b, Individual k's and IRA. They can all be created in Traditional or ROTH form. Your employer may not elect to have ROTH options. If the ROTH option is important to you and it is not offered at work, it is available through most financial firms in the IRA format. You need to check with your financial professional to ask if these plans can be helpful to you.

If you are self-employed, you have an advantage when it comes to your retirement plan. SEPs, Simples, Individual k's and IRAs can be ROTH or Traditional. You get to decide. One again, consult with your tax pro. There is much more flexibility with investment options in these plans, and they often have larger contribution limits. In certain situations the government allows up to $64,000 a year in deductible contributions. That's tax-sheltered money, a benefit that's hard to beat.

The danger for self-employed entrepreneurs is they're often so consumed with planning for their business that they forget to plan for themselves. As a business owner, your retirement savings plan options are better than those of an employee. But you don't benefit at all if you don't take the time to execute them.

YOUR EMERGENCY FUND

You will have emergencies. We all do. An emergency fund protects your retirement savings, so you won't have to prematurely withdraw funds and subject them to penalties and tax.

As a rule, your emergency fund ought to equal three to six months of your expenses. As a rule, the more secure your job is the less you need in your fund. But because the business world has become increasingly volatile, who knows what job is secure. So, I suggest your goal is to have six months of expenses in your fund.

Your emergency fund isn't money to be invested, but money held where you can get to it quickly. Have an emergency checking or savings account, put money in a safe deposit box, hide it under the mattress, or bury it in a coffee can. Just be sure it's available when unexpected trouble strikes; and it will.

Your emergency fund becomes a lifetime balancing act. As you get older, your expenses will increase and there will be times that you need to dip into the emergency or "rainy day" fund. Keep track of this and increase your emergency fund as your expenses increase.

Once you have three months of expenses in the emergency fund, monthly savings can be partially diverted for a major purchase like a home or car. But it's up to you to make sure your emergency account stays fully funded.

If you've been saving for a major purchase, you're in a position of strength. The ability to pay for something in full, saves on interest charges and may give you negotiating leverage. If you have a large down payment on something you need to finance, a new truck for example, a sizable down payment reduces the interest you pay. The loan will be smaller, and you may create a shorter payment term. Having a larger initial deposit can help get a loan approved and with better terms.

The benefit of a larger down payment is even more important when buying a house. When taking a mortgage for a house, if you lack 20% to put down, a thing called Private Mortgage Insurance gets automatically added to your loan. It increases your cost and raises your monthly payments until you have 20% equity in the home.

Once you are in a position of 20% equity in your home, don't expect the mortgage company to come knocking on your door to remove this extra expense. They will be glad to have you continue paying for this extra protection. You're in charge so chase the mortgage company or the insurance provider to get that insurance removed from your basic policy.

Life events like weddings, college, and vacations are inevitable. These are all wonderful provided you live within your means. I hope this book reaches younger readers and helps them be sensitive to the pressure placed on parents to fund these events. A month doesn't go by that someone isn't calling me seeking guidance on how to dig out from a history of extravagant spending now that they are ready to retire. My answer is usually the same, and it's never something they want to hear. The only solution is that they have go back to work.

So, we've talked about the importance for retirement saving. Now the million-dollar question is, how do you do it? The answer is forced savings. The mechanics are simple.

If your employer has a retirement plan, your contributions must go from your paycheck directly into your savings plan. If it's done automatically, you never see the money and get used to living without out. If they don't have a retirement plan, create your own forced savings program with automatic withdrawals from your checking account into one of the recommended plans we've talked about.

Use a checking account to pay your bills and receive your paycheck. Set it up to electronically receive and automatically make payments. It will provide a record of everything coming in and going out, and make bill paying easy. Create automatic transfers every month from your checking account to:

- an IRA account,
- your savings account,
- your emergency fund,
- or a large purchase fund.

I know what you are thinking. I'll make those transfers myself when I have money in the account. Trust me. That won't work for most of us. Set up the forced savings accounts and let them run. If you do get into financial stress, your emergency funds will be there to pay the bills. The IRA account should not be touched.

9

Saving and Investing

Saving is the act of holding aside the difference between what you earn and what you spend. Making this action intentional and proactive is a key to building wealth.

Investing is the act of spending that money you saved on things that you expect to increase in value, provide dividends, or interest.

Of course you need to save or acquire money before you invest it. An important consideration before investing is to have the cash you need to fund monthly expenses. I often say, "never make yourself cash poor". You will have bills and expenses and you need to keep enough money in the account to cover them.

Interest returns on safe savings like a bank savings account are poor and getting worse. If you take the current return on money market accounts and adjust for inflation, clearly the purchasing power of your savings declines every year assuming interest rates stay the same. That said, a money market account is ideal for funds you'll need in the near future.

Retirement savings are completely different than emergency fund savings. As a younger person, the greatest advantage you have is a long investment horizon. Yet many people waste the opportunity. The first step is having money to invest it. Hopefully you are starting on that already. The second step is to take intelligent risks and to be aggressive in your investing. There will be ups and downs in the markets over the next forty years, and since you don't need your retirement funds for a long time, you can withstand that volatility.

Volumes have been written on how to invest money, and there are countless hours of advice on television. The correct answers will only be proven with time, and they will change over time. It is easy to have too much info on this and get paralyzed by it. The industry term for it is 'paralysis by analysis'.

Staying in cash is fine in your emergency fund, but it's a mistake in your long term retirement account. If you have a 401k, it will likely offer Target Dated Funds or Equity Index Funds. The further away the date of a target-dated fund is from today, the more aggressive it will be. Hopefully your retirement plan provider will be able to guide you. And any investment solution you decide on for now is likely to change over time.

Since you are contributing to your retirement account every month now, make sure it gets invested every month. This is called systematic investing and is easily set up by your financial advisor. When markets dip, and they will, do not stop investing. Keep a long-time investment horizon. It has been proven time and again that staying disciplined and not panicking in a down market pays off.

The risk vs return analysis is an important part of any investment decision. In theory the less risky the investment, the less your return. For example, if we compare CD rates currently at 1.5% to certain Hi Yield debt at 11.5%, there is an obvious and significant difference in the return.

"I take it your portfolio is doing well?"

The CD in this discussion is FDIC insured so there is essentially no risk of not getting your investment returned. A Hi Yield bond is subject to a number of market conditions, and there may be a possibility that the borrower will default on all or a portion of the loan. The question then becomes, "Do you have the risk appetite or enough knowledge about the investment to be comfortable with the risk for the extra return?"

Return free risk is a term that is being used more often in the investment world. The term refers to investments that put you at risk but don't provide a return. You would never intentionally enter into something that provides risk without reward, but it happens every day. With our CD returning 1.5% and inflation at 2.5%, the real return on investment is a negative 1%. That is not a good idea, and why it is suggested that CD's should not be your long-term investment vehicle. They are great for short term use when you have to hold the money for a short time period.

The risk vs return analysis should be used daily in many of the decisions you make. In this time of the Covid virus, there is great debate about wearing a mask. Since masks don't cause the disease, there is no risk and they may help prevent the spread of the disease. So there is potential for huge return.

Another example is the friend who needs to borrow your car because his is in the body shop. After totaling his first car, his second one is in for repair. Logic quickly determines you don't want this guy driving your car. The best that can happen is that you'll get the car back in the same condition that you loaned it. The worst case scenario is that your car will wind up in the body shop stall alongside his.

A final example proving the supply of idiots is endless recently happened in California. During this horrible drought and amongst repeated warnings of high fire risk, a couple decided to have a gender reveal party with fireworks for the reveal. 7,000 acres have been burned, and at this writing, the fire is only 3% contained. Homes are being destroyed and lives could be lost. Forgetting the hardship they created for others, the party-goers will suffer emotionally and financially for the rest of their lives. So, for the risk of harming others and devastating their own finances, this couple sought the reward of entertaining their friends with fireworks. Bad decision.

I briefly mentioned inflation earlier this chapter and it needs more attention. Inflation means the items you buy costs more than it once did. This makes the buying power of your dollar less every year. While the hope of investing is to grow assets significantly, a minimum goal is to stay current with inflation.

10

Savings Vehicles vs. Investment Vehicles

Once again there is an endless supply of advice on investing. My goal is to acquaint you with the basics. The three usual categories are cash, stocks or equities, and bonds.

Cash can be in all forms: the green stuff, a savings account, a money market account, or the balance in your check book. Cash provides accesses to funds with no risk of loss. Cash is often held while in anticipation of buying other investments in the future. But remember that when you hold cash, you'll almost never outpace inflation. So, your dollars are worth less as time goes by. In the '70s I was proud that my money market account was earning 12%. What I failed to recognize was that inflation was closer to 18%. I was losing 6% of buying power a year.

When you invest in **stocks or equities,** in theory you own a small slice of the company. You select the stocks you purchase based on a bet that companies will grow in size and value. There's a lot of research and science available when you make your selection, but simple observation can be just as productive. The return from a growing company is usually greater than inflation which is why you use stocks to grow your portfolio.

Stock prices fluctuate based on logic and emotion. If a company is successful and shows success on its financial statements, then logically its value will increase. Investors will be comfortable to pay more for that stock. However, stocks will fluctuate based on all kinds of things you have no control over. For example, suppose the president of that company does something that gets bad press. Even though the company has been financially successful up until now, the stock price could fall.

Emotion plays as big a role in the pricing of stocks as does logic. And emotion is difficult to measure. Moods, rumors, current events can all improperly run up or run down the price of a stock. As a small investor, you can't control these factors, but be aware they are always operating, and that people's emotions can create risk or opportunity.

Bonds represent the debt of a company. When you purchase a bond, you're lending the company money. The company that issues the bond owes you for that share of their debt. The theory behind bonds is that they are more secure than stocks and provide a better yield than cash.

Bonds have long been a stable investment used to reduce risk and provide return through dividends. With interest rates so low at the time I'm writing this, bonds may be less attractive as a stable investment that provides return.

Investing in stocks is challenging because you need to pick companies that will grow and increase in value. The value of bonds is more likely to fluctuate based on current interest rates. Investing in either involves risk weighted against reward. It may be worth getting investment guidance from professional sources whom you trust. They can best help you see the pros and risks for the investment you're considering.

The current low interest rate environment increases the potential volatility of a bond investment. As an example, let's say we both purchased a 10-year, $10,000 treasury bond last year. The yield on your bond was 1%, and I bought mine a month later at a yield of 1.5%. Assume we each hold our bonds for 2 years and decide to sell them when the rate of treasuries is 2%.

Since bond buyers can obtain new bonds at the higher rate of 2%, nobody will want to buy the ones we hold for the $10,000 we paid. In order to sell our bonds, we will need to discount our price to make them competitive. The difference in the rate for our bond times the number of years left to maturity will give you an idea of how big the discount has to be to sell it. In our example, you would need to reduce the selling price of your bond by 1% times 8 years or $800. I would need to reduce the price of mine by .5% times 8 years or $400.

The purpose of this example is to show that even though 10-year treasury bonds are considered one of the safest investments in the world, you can lose money on them. Outside influences like yield rates can affect demand for a bond.

Corporate bonds are those issued by companies. Municipal bonds are those issued by cities, towns, and states. The US government issues Treasury bonds. You can buy bonds directly from the issuer, or through Mutual Funds, ETF's, or other investment vehicles. You can buy them with different maturities (long term, intermediate, or short duration). They can be purchased with higher risk which provides a larger dividend, but there is a greater potential to lose part or all of your investment.

Bonds are an investment class to consider in your portfolio, but you need to recognize that the good ones may be more difficult to select than good stocks.

When investing, you can buy and hold shares of an individual company stock or bond. Doing so allows you to be very selective and to own exactly what you want. But for those who are risk-adverse or lack the expertise to pick individual stocks, vehicles like Mutual Funds and ETF's (Exchange Traded Funds) come into play.

A Mutual fund has teams of managers and researchers that help them pick investments that are appropriate for their fund. For example, if the fund holds Corporate Bonds, that will be the key focus for the fund's investment experts. Or if the goal of the fund is to own Technology, the bulk of the team's research will study technology companies.

When you buy shares of the fund, you participate in its performance (growth or loss). In theory, by having expert fund managers and researchers, they will do a better job of selecting what companies to invest in. This doesn't always work of course, so you need to watch their performance.

Exchange Traded Funds or ETF's have grown in popularity. Originally these funds provided no benefit of management or research, but that's changing and many now provide research investment selection at a low cost. They can be good investment vehicle if you take the time to learn about the companies a particular fund holds.

Real Estate Trusts (REITS), Business Development Companies (BDCs), Master Limited Partnerships (MLPs) are also potential investment vehicles and provide access to specific markets. They are created by legislation that requires that 90% of their income be distributed to shareholders. They can offer higher yields but can be illiquid (not easy to sell). They are usually appropriate only for a knowledgeable investor.

Change is the only constant in the investment world. I've listed a few of the ways to invest. There are more, and new ones will always arrive. Keep learning and looking for the opportunities that are right for you.

Bitcoin and the crypto currencies have burst onto the investment scene. While they are called currencies, the volatility of their pricing makes them act like a stock. Because the crypto currencies don't produce a product (like merchandise or a service), it is difficult to value them the way you value stock.

Option trading is another vehicle and popular with new investors because of online trading apps. Options make or destroy fortunes and can do so quickly. Options can also provide increased protection to your portfolio or offer leveraged returns if used properly. I like options as a part of most portfolios, but incredible diligence is required if you use them.

> Recently a college student who was using a free trading app created a several hundred-thousand-dollar loss with an option trade. He took his life as a result. The free app he used did not demand the licensing and education that a financial professional is required to have to make much smaller and less complex trades. Hopefully by the time you read this the rules will have changed, but remember that just because you can do something, it may not be a good idea.

Many fortunes are made investing in Real Estate. While larger sums of money are usually required to invest, you can invest directly in Real Estate through stocks or REIT's. I often hear people say, "You can't lose money with Real Estate." Please be cautious if you think that's true. As with any investment, outside factors can affect real estate value. As an example though New York real estate had been on a 10-year positive track since 2009, the Covid virus is significantly depressing prices. Or, layoffs from the largest employer in any town will hurt real-estate pricing. Increases in interest rates can hurt the real estate market.

Disasters create opportunity. You don't want to be the restaurant owner selling your property at fire sale prices due to the Covid. But if you wanted to buy a restaurant, now may be the time. While you never wish anyone harmed by disasters, they can create advantage for someone else, and business is business.

11

Taxes

As sure as the sun will rise, after you join the working world, taxes will be a favorite topic. They are the price we pay to live in our society whether we agree with how the government spends our tax dollars or not.

On more than one occasion I've had young professionals ask to discuss how their employer is stealing from them. "My check was supposed to be for $1,000 and I only got $743." A quick estimate paying 12% in federal tax, 6% for state tax, 6.2% for your share of payroll tax, and 1.45% medicare tax, usually identifies where the "stolen" money has gone.

After explaining taxes, their next statement is also predictable. "That's not fair. I earned that money." Once again welcome to the real world. All government programs must be funded, and you're now part of the source of funding. Their next question is, "How do I avoid paying taxes?"

"And what will you gentlemen be writing off this evening?"

For the typical worker, the best bet is to contribute to a retirement account. Doing so reduces your taxable income. Some will ask, "What about getting paid 'under the table?'" Now there's a strategy that can put you in jail. Furthermore, your Social Security retirement and disability benefits are calculated from the income you declare. Maximizing your retirement and disability credits are important for your financial future.

Taxes can be charged to you on the local, state, and federal level. Local taxes are usually not on income but on your property like a car or home. Some larger cities will charge an income tax. Keep that in mind if you are taking a new job in a big city. It will cost more to live there so you need to get paid more.

State taxes are charged by the state you live in. This has caused recent concern as now that much work is done virtually you can move to a no tax state and save thousands. State governments will lose massive tax income because of this new dynamic and likely figure out some way to collect. For now, this can be a savings opportunity.

> This Could Be Significant. The idea of working virtually from a tax free state is a concept I have reviewed with many friends. In one case the tax savings was so significant that over a period of 15 years it would completely pay for the new home in Florida.

Federal taxes are the ones you will hear about the most. These pay for all the government programs that support our society. I am a big fan of helping others but concerned about the over graciousness of our politicians.

Politicians tend to get elected based on how much they "give" to their voters. What seems to get lost is the taxpayers need to fund all this financial support. Younger people like yourself will bear most of the burden to pay for gracious government spending as you have 40-plus years of taxable earnings. Those doing all the giving have much fewer years and may benefit politically from their graciousness with your money.

I make no claims that the spending choices of our government are good or bad. But you will be paying for most of them, so pay attention and have a voice when you can.

12

The Why and When of Insurance

'Not Sexy.' That's the best description I know of for insurance in the financial world. And if it is done right, it will stay 'not sexy'. While many kinds of insurance can be used as investment vehicles, consider insurance chiefly as a "sleep-at-night" expense. I have older friends who've never paid for anything more than state mandated auto insurance. Basically, they self-insured, and it worked in their cases. Many had significant wealth and could cover themselves in the event of a catastrophe. But I wouldn't suggest living that way.

Many years ago, the company I worked for hired a bright young mechanic. He was a great guy and has been a friend for years. About a month after hiring him, we received notice from the court to garnish 20% of his wages. His money was to be sent to the person he hurt in an automobile accident which he caused since he had no insurance. It took ten years of garnished wages to pay off those damages.

Auto insurance is the most common insurance and it's required if you have a loan on your vehicle. States have different laws, but all of them require some type of liability insurance, and that's a good thing to avoid what happened to my friend. Had there been a death or disability from his accident, he might be paying for it for the rest of his life.

Insurance deductibles or how much you pay on a claim before insurance covers the rest will vary. Higher deductibles mean lower insurance premiums (premium is the fancy insurance term for 'cost'). Lower deductible will increase the cost of your insurance. You need to decide on how much risk you can take based on how much money you have to cover the deductible should you have an accident.

There are two parts to auto insurance. Liability covers the cost of harm you do to someone else. Collision covers the cost of repairing your own vehicle. If you are driving an old car of little value, you might want to drop collision insurance, but keep in mind if you wreck the car, you'll get nothing to help buy another one.

Remember that your credit score can affect how much your insurance costs. I don't claim to understand how this is determined, but keeping good credit saved me a bunch. Pay your bills on time and it will save on your insurance policy.

Homeowners insurance covers damage to your home while protecting you from liability if someone is harmed on your property. Your mortgage provider will require this, and you want to speak with your insurance agent about deductibles. He or she can advise on and how much coverage you should have and can afford.

A lesser-known insurance policy is called an Umbrella policy. These cover you from excess liability should a bad injury occur to someone when you are responsible. Umbrella policies are usually available in million-dollar coverage increments and may be added to your home or auto insurance policy. The probability that you will ever need this is exceptionally low, so the cost is usually very reasonable. Talk to your agent about this.

Life insurance can do a lot of things. A policy providing a death benefit is the most common, and can act as an estate planning tool, a college fund or provide long-term health care protection. Let's keep things simple and focus on life insurance as a vehicle for protecting your family in the event of your death.

An unplanned death means the loss of your income for those you leave behind. That's what creates hardship. The classic example is a couple with two kids, a mortgage, and hopes for the kids to get a higher education. Assuming both spouses work, earn the same income, the household will lose 50% of its income with the loss of a spouse.

Take, for example, a case where you make $80,000 a year. Assume, should you die, that you want to be able to pay off a $300,000 house mortgage while providing for your spouse until your youngest, age four, is out of college. You'll need 17 times $80,000 plus $300,000. That comes to a total of $1,660,000 - the amount of insurance coverage you need.

It seems like a lot of money, and it is. But even this simple formula doesn't cover some of the other calculations you need to factor in. For example, your $80,0000 income is subject to tax while your insurance benefit is not. The calculation also doesn't account for the fact that your mortgage balance gets smaller every year you survive. The point is that there are many insurance options to consider. Work with an insurance agent you trust to determine the right amount of coverage and the best policy options.

There are two types of life insurance, and the one I suggest for many family situations is convertible term. In the case of term insurance, you're betting the insurance company you'll die within the specified policy period. The insurance company bets that you won't. The convertible part of the insurance means that you can convert term to a permanent policy in the future. You want to be sure the conversion feature stays in place for the length of the term policy, which is typically 10, 15, or 20 years.

The ability to convert a term policy to a permanent policy is a benefit in the event a bad health issue arises during the time you own the term policy. For example, let's say you bought a 15 year term policy with a $1.5 million dollar death benefit. 14 years from now you discover you have cancer, and only a few years to live. At this point you are uninsurable from any company. However, with a convertible term policy, you can convert it to a permanent one, keep making payments and have insurance to protect your family. Be assured the cost to keep your benefit at $1.5 million will

"Yes Sir, all our flambe dishes come with liability insurance."

increase. But, you can continue your coverage, and the benefit to your family may be massive.

The other type of insurance is called permanent insurance. It stays in place for your lifetime provided you keep making payments. The death benefit for a permanent policy vs a term policy costs more, reflecting the greater risk to the insurance company. Permanent policies also work well as tax-sheltered investment vehicles under some circumstances. They can also be a tax efficient way to build retirement savings, but only after your maximum retirement account annual contributions have been reached.

Advanced insurance strategies require guidance from a financial professional. Caution is needed as this is a high commission product. When used properly insurance will benefit you. But if used improperly, they won't be cost effective. Banks love to sell insurance and less stringent fiduciary rules may apply. So be careful.

13

Buying VS Leasing a Car

The decision to buy or lease a car depends on your personal situation and the amount of lease incentive provided by the vehicle manufacturer.

A famous television financial advisor is quick to state that you should never lease a car. Be careful with the word *never,* and let's look a little deeper. She stated she had leased a car that was too expensive for her to buy in order to impress someone. She also had to pay an excess mileage charge at the end of the lease.

Mileage charges are a hot spot when it comes to leasing. The ads you see are almost always based on low mileage plans. If you drive 20,000 miles a year and lease a car for 10,000 miles a year, you'll get crushed with mileage charges.

"Our computer shows you have a weak battery, bad plugs and you're four days late on your auto loan payment."

If you drive 20,000 miles a year, get the lease calculated for 20,000 miles per year. This will give you a more accurate picture of what the lease really costs. Don't be afraid to put extra miles in a lease. We paid for extra miles on my wife's sports car at 10 cents per mile. That is cheaper than the depreciation for excess miles on the car if we owned it.

Money down on a lease lowers the monthly payment, but all you are doing is prepaying for the use of the car. This makes the monthly payment look better, but once again you are fooling yourself. You end up paying just as much.

> A friend leased a Yukon Denali several years ago. They drove 25,000 miles per year, and to keep the lease consistent with their use I had them buy the extra miles at 15 cents per mile. Luxury vehicles depreciated at that time at about 30 cents per excess mile, so this seemed like a bargain. It was and the lease company lost over $10,000 when they sold the truck at the completion of the lease. (It is not your job to protect the lease company.) On completion of the Denali lease, my friend needed another truck. The lease deals were not attractive, and the purchase offers were compelling. So this time they opted to purchase the vehicle.

Since the main components of a lease are interest expense and depreciation, market conditions can make a difference. Lease interest is calculated in a more complex way than simple loan interest, but it provides a lower rate which can be misleading. In addition, a robust or weak demand for off-lease cars can also affect the future value of the vehicle making the depreciation you pay greater or smaller.

The decision to lease or purchase is driven by your needs. If you are getting a pickup you intend to have for 10 years, and you're a little rough on your vehicles, leasing is just not a good idea. You'll get hit with high turn-in charges. If you are looking at a sports car to use for a couple of years, leasing may be a good idea.

Some manufacturers tend to have better leases than others, and some models offer better lease values than others. First, chose the vehicle that best fits your needs, then figure the best way to obtain it. Picking the wrong vehicle will make you trade sooner which creates more expense. Keep in mind the right answer for your current vehicle may not be the right answer for your next. Do your homework as vehicles are amongst the larger financial decisions you'll make.

Purchasing a new vehicle is exciting and emotional but, do the math and make the most rational decision. Most manufacturers let you choose a rebate or a low interest rate when purchasing. The rate may look attractive but keep thinking.

Suppose you are buying a car for $33,000 and have the choice of 0% financing for 60 months or a $3,000 rebate. Let's assume you put $3,000 down. If you take the rebate and put down $3,000, you will be financing $27,000 at 3%. If you make all payments on time your interest expense is approximately $2,0000. Taking the rebate, you also reduce the taxable price of the sale. My state charges 7%, so using that as an example, there is a $210 tax savings.

Let's review. After you deduct the interest expense from the rebate, you save almost $1,000. Add to that the $210 tax savings, and you've saved a total of $1,185. That is real money that can be saved or enjoyed.

Finance Amount	Finance cost	Total Cost
$30,000 @ 0% for 60 months	$0	$30,000
$27,000@ 3% for 60 months	$2025	$29,025

Let's flip things for a minute and assume you didn't follow my advice to pay your bills on time and your credit is poor. Let's also say that the non-incentivized interest rate is 6%, not 3%. Now you have approximately $4,500 in interest costs, so the factory subsidized 0% starts to look good.

Shop around for car loans as lenders use different approval criteria. It is not uncommon for one source to have a much better rate than another. Be warned. If you let your credit get bad, interest charges can soar to as much as 21%. Or you might not get a loan at all.

Just last week I bumped into an old friend who is the finance manager at a dealership that specializes in helping people with bad credit. I had to ask him what the average rate was that those clients were paying. The answer was 18%. You can avoid that huge expense by paying your bills on time.

14

Buying a Home vs Renting

There are advantages and disadvantages to both. Once again, your personal situation will dictate what the best choice for you would be. When I worked for General Motors, the field employees got moved a lot — sometimes on a yearly basis. I remember my friend Larry who I mentioned in a previous chapter getting moved from Texas to Boston. Home prices in Boston were astronomical at the time and two years later when Larry got promoted and moved, he lost tens of thousands of dollars on the sale of his home.

Conversely, the gentleman who Larry replaced moved to a state with a depressed housing market. That market recovered while he was there, and he not only made a bundle when selling that home, but he moved back to Boston when prices crashed and bought his old house back for much less than he had sold it for previously. I share this example to prove that home ownership can be a winner or a loser from a financial perspective.

One of the great arguments for homeownership is you are building equity. This is true and you build equity by making principal payments on your mortgage every month along with the hope that homes in your area will increase in value.

When looking at the monthly cost of renting vs buying, keep in mind that if you own the home you are responsible for taxes, repairs, and insurance. In some cases when you add in all the extra costs of home ownership you might be better renting and saving/investing the difference.

Of course, the security of having control over the place you live is a large benefit, and the flexibility of customizing your living space to your needs is great. I can provide no clear direction on which choice will be best for you but encourage you to think through the options carefully before deciding.

15

Bringing it All Together

You are in charge of you. Be dependable and positive.

After having a little too much fun the night before and needing to be on the job site by 8 am, I'd tell myself I could do it. I made it to work on time and convinced myself that all was just fine. In fact, I wasn't performing at my best.

It is okay to have as much fun as legally possible. It is not acceptable if an employer or others get punished for the fun you had. I missed very few parties, events, and fire brewed beverages, but I never missed a day of work. I always remembered the importance of being a dependable employee. I did show up 45 minutes late one time because I was delayed while being discharged from the emergency room. At least I got a doctor's note. My boss was unhappy about my tardiness but impressed by the fact I left the ER and came directly to work. It got me my next promotion.

Read, *Love Your Enemies* by Arthur Brooks. Brooks is accomplished, smart, and has access to fabulous scientists and leaders. His writings advise that assuming a positive attitude is a good habit to develop. If you're smiling, it will eventually lead to more positive emotions. I'm not a psychologist, but positive people are happier, and attract more friends. A smile costs nothing, and it helps me make and enjoy my friends.

There will be bad days, but don't let them determine who you are. Mothers from past generations would tell their children, "Put on a smile and get back out there." It sounds simple, but it's good advice and it works.

Someone once told me, "You can manage your efforts but not your results." What you do each day will either be productive, nonproductive, or counterproductive. Stay focused on being productive. As a young person starting out, perhaps you should take that low-paying job at $12 an hour while you look for a better opportunity. That's more productive than living off your parents. Save as much as you can so one day you can become independent, start a business, or make a down payment on a house.

Life offers no guarantees, and it's possible to do everything right and still not get ahead. Alternatively, if you do nothing or do everything wrong, you'll have zero chance of success. Be on the lookout for opportunities and take them. Remember what Confucius said, "If we don't change direction, we're liable to end up where we're headed."

Don't bother to worry about things in this world that are beyond your control. Manage the things you can manage. Get to work early and be the best you can be at whatever you do. Make yourself more valuable every day and keep looking for that next opportunity. Never spend money you don't have, on things you don't need, to impress people that don't matter.

The most horrible person I ever worked for taught me one of the greatest lessons. He repeatedly said, "It is not in the best interest of the company," when I suggested changes that would make things better. Under his leadership the company went into bankruptcy. Turn his statement around to, "Is what I am doing right now in the best interest of ___________ (my future, my family, my community, my company)? Use this rule to determine if your current actions are the best use of your time.

I'm not suggesting you shouldn't have fun. Rest and relaxation allow you to perform at your best when it is time to work. Just don't overdo the R&R.

Keep life in perspective. You may know the famous Serenity Prayer from Dr. Reinhold Niebuhr and used by AA. It goes:

"God, grant me the Serenity to Accept the things I cannot change, Courage to change the things I can, and Wisdom to know the difference."

I use the above prayer often but change the last verse to "and give me the strength not to waste my time figuring out how to harm those that make me angry".

Remember the importance of being productive about how you spend your time and energy. Anger and frustration can lead to wasted time and effort. If someone makes you mad, the act of forgiveness is less about being a good person than it is about not wasting your valuable time on people that cause you to be nonproductive.

Financial success is up to you. If you make the effort, if you do the work, if you provide the discipline, the chances of a favorable outcome really increase. Sure, there will be bad days, months, or even years. Keep your head up and keep looking for that next step to improve your position.

Things will happen that are to your disadvantage. Maybe your boss's nephew gets the job you deserve. Maybe your boss is a jerk, or the economy in your town collapses, or you suffer a family illness. That is life and while there will be up and down days, if you stay positive you will live through difficult times and prosper.

I cannot overstate how basic the financial information I have presented to you is or the vast amount of knowledge that needs to be added by you in the future.

So go to work, save a few dollars, make friends, help someone else, avoid an idiot, avoid being an idiot, and learn, learn, learn. There is no magic. It's all up to you, and you can succeed if you do the work. *Best wishes!*

About the Author

Spencer J. Seitz describes himself as "a kid who grew up in a small-town where economic opportunity was limited and success unlikely." But fate, and grit changed all that.

In his early days, the loss of a full ride scholarship for political reasons, and the theft of tens of thousands of dollars by a trusted business associate, provided a foundation to better appreciate the realities of the business world. He confronted those realities again working for challenging employers whose careless management destroyed the businesses. Spencer considers each of those disasters important learning experiences. He found a better way and soon found himself rising up the corporate ladder with a major retailer.

After a decade of success as a corporate executive, Spencer changed careers, fascinated by the opportunities to help with financial planning. He earned licenses on federal and multiple state levels to provide investment advice and financial strategy, obtaining his CRPC certification (Charter Retirement Planning Counselor). Today he revels in helping others reach their financial goals by combining the perspective of risk and the impact of taxes to help build successful estate and retirement plans. As the majority partner of a private wealth advisory practice, Spencer has helped clients increase net worth by millions of dollars.

Now, with a hope to 'pay it forward,' he has written *Basic Common Cent$* to give young people a head start on the road to financial stability. The book introduces them to the basics of finance while encouraging good decision making to achieve financial comfort and peace of mind.

Made in the USA
Monee, IL
04 November 2026

67380407R00046